Little Sprout is dedicated
to my six "little sprouts",
Mitch, Dani, Kaeli, Gabe, Carter, and Averie.

Mom and Gami love you all!

I'm a little sprout!

I'm growing up and out!

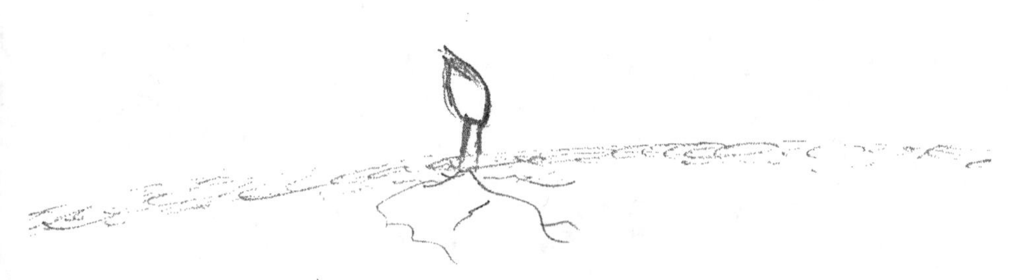

*color the sprout green, and dirt brown

I'm out of the ground!

I'm out and abound!

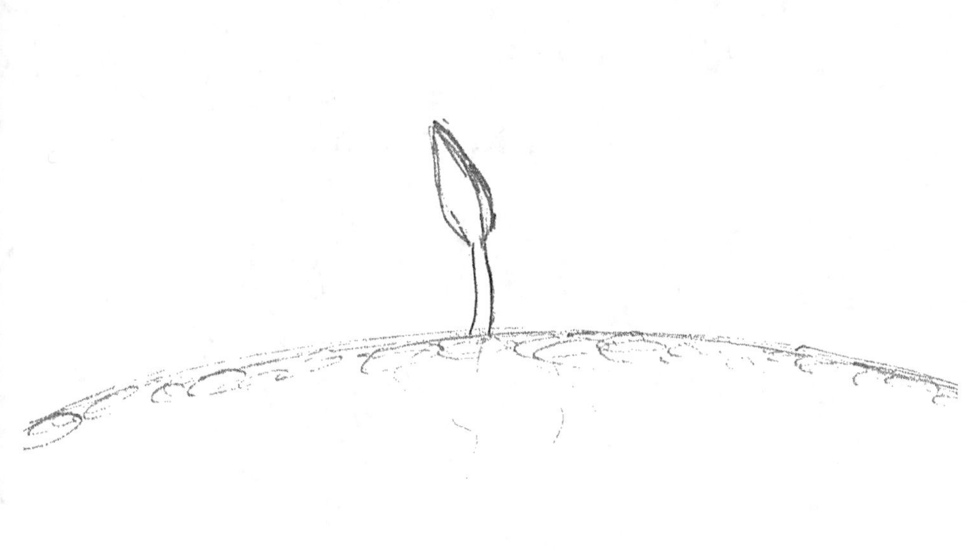

*color the sprout green, dirt brown and sky blue

I'm still a little small!

I'm going to grow tall!

*color the sprout green, dirt brown, sky blue,
and trace the roots

What will I become?

What colors will I be?

*color the sprout green, dirt brown, sky blue,
trace the roots and clouds

My leaves are green!

My stem is green too!

*color the sprout green, dirt brown, trace the
roots and clouds, color the grass and leaves green

Will I stay this way?

Will I stay just green?

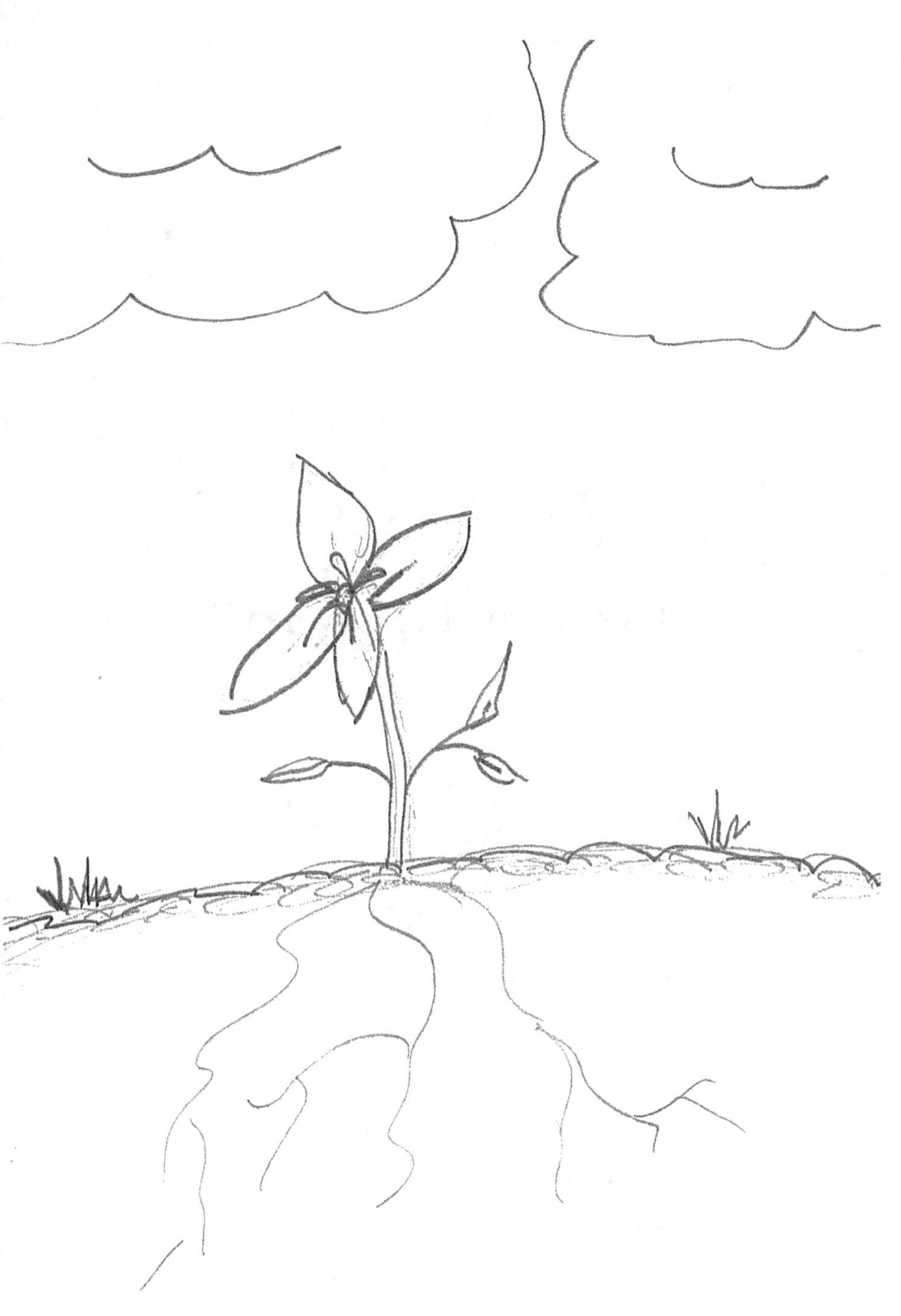

*color the sprout, leaves, stem and grass green,
trace the roots and clouds

I see some color!

There is color on my head!

*color leaves, stem, grass and outside flower leaves green, color the center of the flower yellow, trace roots and clouds and color the dirt brown

I'm yellow and green!

These are the colors I shall be!

*color leaves, stem, grass and outside of the
circle green, color the center of and
first row yellow, trace roots and clouds
and color the dirt brown

I'm so excited to be
something more than green!

*color leaves and stem green, sky blue
and flower petals yellow, center of the
circle will have black dots

Look, I'm smiling at the sun!

I'm happy as can be!

*color stem and leaves green, sun and flower
petals yellow, trace the clouds,
center of the circle will have black dots

I'm a sunflower!

I'm as bright as they come!

*color the flower yellow, center will have black
dots, stem and leaves green, sky will be blue
and trace the clouds

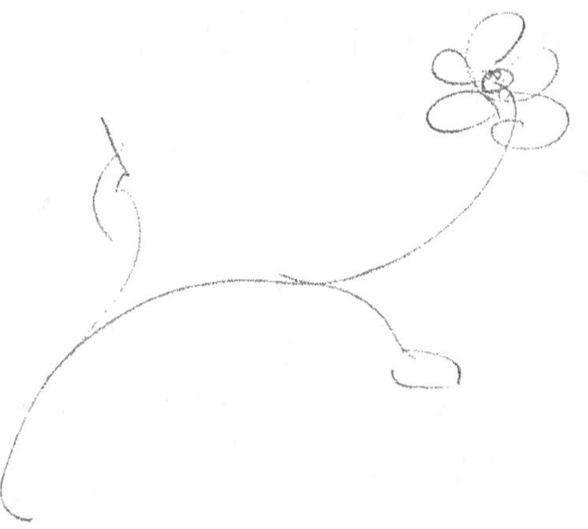

The
End . . . .

My Name is _________________________________

I colored my book _____ /_____/_____

I am ________ Years Old